Mind Power

A Practical Guide To Learn How Mind And Subconscious Are Related

Ian Berry

Table Of Contents

Introduction

Sigmund Freud, the father of psychoanalysis, was among the first people in the world to talk about human personality and the way our mind is structured. He was the one to introduce the three important structures: conscious, subconscious and unconscious mind. Today, we have come a long way from those times and we definitely know a lot more information on how the mind functions and the way these three structures are interconnected.

In this book, you will find exciting information on how the mind and the subconscious are related. Moreover, you will be able to find out about the power of the conscious mind and the important role the unconscious plays in the whole picture. The fantastic read introduces you into the world of thoughts, presents visualization as a unique technique to stimulate mind power and also provides a glimpse into the laws of attraction. It is a wonderful reading experience and one that will leave you feeling richer in the end.

Here is a preview of what you are going to discover in the book:

- Functions of the conscious mind

- Role of the subconscious mind

- Unconscious mind and psychological repression

- The power of positive thinking

- Visualization techniques

- Mind power and the law of attraction

- The most common myths and misconceptions regarding mind power

- And many more...

Use this book as your guideline regarding mind power and learn how the mind and the subconscious are related. Make sure to go through all the chapters and enjoy your reading experience, jotting down any information you have considered to be interesting.

Chapter 1 – The conscious mind

Sigmund Freud: "The conscious mind may be compared to a fountain playing in the sun and falling back into the great subterranean pools of subconscious from which it rises."

The conscious mind & awareness

Sigmund Freud was indeed one of the most prolific psychoanalysts of all times, working to shed light on human personality and the role of the conscious mind (in parallel with the subconscious and unconscious). Today, thanks to Mr. Freud and other men of value, we know that the conscious mind includes all the things we are aware of and think about (rationally).

The mental processing connected to the conscious mind is complex and always related to the things that go through our head. Awareness is what keeps us grounded and connected to the daily life; every sensation, perception, memory, sentiment or even fantasy is translated into the conscious mind and forms the way we see the world.

The division of the human personality into subconscious and conscious was a breakthrough for Sigmund Freud (he would go on later, to discover the unconscious as well). It was then that he began to use the iceberg metaphor, in order to describe the two main aspects of the human personality. He called the conscious mind as being the tip of the iceberg, or just what it is visible above the water. What lied beneath, far more complex and with a deeper meaning, was the subconscious.

Some researchers have compared the conscious mind to the short-term memory, as it includes everything we are currently aware of, as well as the things we consciously think about. However, given this comparison, it should also be highlighted that the conscious mind has a limited capacity (as opposed to the subconscious, which researchers have deemed to have a virtually endless capacity).

Preconscious mind

The concept of the preconscious mind belongs to Sigmund Freud as well, referring to all the information that we have stored and we can easily draw into the conscious mind, upon it being necessary. In short, it refers to the information we possess but we are not necessarily thinking about at that respective moment. The preconscious mind is closely related to the conscious mind.

Functions of the conscious mind

According to researchers, the conscious mind presents a number of essential functions.

The first function is related to the identification of information that comes our way. This information can be received through any of six senses – feeling, touching, tasting, smelling, hearing or seeing – as the conscious mind is actively busy in analyzing the environment and what is happening to us.

Let's take a practical example, in order to better understand this first function. Imagine yourself wanting to cross the street and hearing the engine of a car. You will automatically turn your head in the direction of the car, in order to identify how close that car is actually to you.

The second function is represented by comparison. Continuing with the example above, once you have seen the car, the mind will begin to compare it with previous experiences (these are stored and retrieved from the subconscious). In this way, you can determine whether you are in real danger or not.

The third function is analysis, the conscious mind being involved in an active process of deciding what choice should be made. In a similar manner to a computer, it will determine whether it is safe for you to cross the street, at that point, or not. The conscious mind will always take the best decision for you, based on the need for safety and protection.

Last, but not least, you have the fourth function, which is represented by the taking of the final decision. After analyzing the information received and comparing it to previously stored experiences, the conscious mind will help you cross the street in safety.

What can you learn from the conscious mind?

Even though a lot of attention has been dedicated to the subconscious mind, it is essential to understand and remember that the conscious mind plays an important part as well. It can help you reach the point you want in your life, as you are the only person who is responsible for the creation of your own thoughts and actions.

It is because of the conscious mind that you are able to follow your best intensions, developing a correct understanding about life and the things you want to focus upon, for the years to come. In fact, the subconscious mind will help you develop beneficial life strategies, form relationships that will benefit you on a long-term basis and become more aware of who you are.

Interestingly enough, the conscious mind can help you manage the fears set deep within the subconscious. You are the only one who can acknowledge and manage your fears, so do not hesitate to put your conscious mind to good use. It might interest you to know that the conscious mind is the best source of positive energy, allowing you to stay grounded and aware of the present.

From what has been said up to this point, you have probably understood that the conscious mind plays a number of essential roles in our daily existence. It is because of the conscious mind that we are able to experience the physical world, becoming aware of the things that are happening around us. It is the conscious mind that separates us from the rest of the beings on this planet, demonstrating our complex creation.

Food for thought

1) Try to imagine a situation in which all of the functions of the conscious mind apply.

2) Do you believe that the conscious mind is a big or a small part of your personality?

3) How would you describe the conscious mind, using one single sentence?

Chapter 2 – The subconscious mind

Robert Collier: "Our subconscious minds have no sense of humor, play no jokes and cannot tell the difference between reality and imagined thought or image. What we continually think about eventually will manifest in our lives."

For Sigmund Freud, the subconscious mind was the part of the iceberg, which was subdued in water and hidden to the eye. According to modern research, the subconscious mind can be easily compared to a memory bank, which virtually has no limits. All the things you have gone through, all the information accumulated, experiences – everything is stored in the subconscious mind.

The subconscious mind has represented a subject of interest for a lot of scientists and researchers out there. It is said that a single person will accumulate a hundred times more information, than the one contained in the whole Encyclopedia Britannica, before reaching the age of twenty-one. Other studies, based on hypnosis, have revealed that people are able to recall information, despite it being 50 years old, with uttermost precision. This is because the information stored in the subconscious mind remains intact and stored in there, until we need it again.

What is the main function of the subconscious mind? Well, it is exactly the storage and retrieval of information. However, this does not occur randomly but rather in accordance to your pre-programmed personality. Once you have reached a certain age, you have already developed the self concept and the subconscious mind will always try to get you to behave, in accordance to the way you have programmed yourself.

It is quite obvious that the subconscious mind is subjective, following the orders given by the conscious mind. It is not capable of independent thinking or reasoning, hence the need to obey the conscious one. In a way, you can look at the conscious mind as a gardener, who is carefully planting seeds in his garden, meaning the subconscious mind.

The subconscious mind is active at all times, so as to make sure that you do not stray from your programmed behavior. Consistency is an important matter for the subconscious mind, as it works hard to ensure that your actions are consistent with your thoughts, desires and hopes. Returning to the garden/gardener analogy, the subconscious mind will grow what you have planted in the garden, either flowers or weeds.

From a pragmatic point of view, the subconscious mind plays another important role and that is to keep you alive. This is known as the homeostatic impulse and it ensures that your body temperature, breathing and heart beat rate stay at a normal and healthy level. So, you see, the subconscious mind is responsible for maintaining the balance or harmony within your body.

The subconscious mind is where your past is stored. It has a huge responsibility, in the sense that it has to maintain the same line of thinking and behaviors as in the past. All of your habits are stored in the subconscious mind, being brought to the surface by the conscious mind (remember the four essential functions and the example given, with you having to cross the street).

The fact that the subconscious mind is able to retrieve stored information is not always a good thing. This is because the subconscious mind has made a note of all your comfort zones, working really hard that you do not go over the set borders. In the situation that you want to try new experiences or go in a different direction, than your pre-programmed self, the subconscious will be activated. It will cause discomforting emotional and physical symptoms, in order to make you quit these new things and stick to your established pattern of behavior. Sometimes, the subconscious is so powerful, that you can literally feel the way you are pulled back towards the comfort zone.

We have already established that the mind functions in a similar manner to a computer, having three important segments: conscious, subconscious and unconscious. With regard to the subconscious, it is only normal to ask yourself: can I reprogram it? Well, the answer is yes. You can reprogram your subconscious mind and change established patterns of behavior. At the same time, you can reprogram it, so that you extend your comfort zones or increase the rate of acceptance for new experiences.

Let's say that the subconscious mind is a computer. Well, all you have to do is install the new programs you want, in that part of the computer. In this way, you can overcome your features, fix personality problems and make a change for the better. You might not be aware of this but you can program your subconscious with the help of hypnosis; what matters is that you place yourself in the hands of an experienced hypnotist.

Why does the subconscious mind work so hard to keep us within our comfort zones? Well, according to the research made in the field, it is the most important line of defense against any kind of shock or wound. Whenever we are going to attempt something new or different, the ego defense mechanisms of the subconscious mind will fall into place. These are meant to protect us, against harmful emotions, shocks or wounds.

There is one more very important thing that you should remember about the subconscious mind. It learns through repetition and it does not follow any logic or reasoning. So, if we were to return for one brief moment to the gardening metaphor, it does matter what you put in your garden. If your subconscious mind is only filled with negative thoughts, it is highly likely you will perceive life from the same perspective.

The good news is that you can reprogram the subconscious mind and escape the pattern of negative thinking. In fact, the successful reprogramming can help you make a genuine change in your life, embracing things more openly and showing yourself interested in new experiences.

Food for thought

1) Name three ways in which the subconscious mind can be controlled

2) How does the subconscious mind different from the conscious one?

3) How can success be achieved, through the reprogramming of the subconscious mind?

Chapter 3 – The unconscious mind

Carl Jung: "The unconscious mind of man sees correctly even when conscious reason is blind and impotent."

The unconscious mind includes automatic thought processes, without these being available for introspection. Apart from that, this part of mind includes all the memories we have gathered throughout the years, our interests and the things that motivate us. It represents home for all of feelings we have repressed, for automatic skills, reactions and habits, as well as for fears, desires and phobia. As you will have the opportunity to read below, it is our very own Pandora box.

Sigmund Freud and his views on the unconscious mind

According to the great psychoanalyst, the things we have stored in the unconscious mind will almost always make it into the limelight, either in the form of dreams, jokes or even slips of the tongue.

The unconscious mind is the primary source of dreams, as well as of thoughts, which occur in an automatic manner. Memories we might have forgotten about and accumulated knowledge are stored in the unconscious as well. Automatic skills and habits are there as well, just in case we might need them again, at some point in our lives.

Sigmund Freud, in developing his theories about human personality, proposed a hierarchical structure for the human consciousness. The levels included the conscious, pre-conscious and unconscious mind, all standing on top of each other and having a definite influence on one another. For example, it is clear that the conscious mind is influenced by the unconscious, especially with regard to our habits or desires.

The psychoanalyst spent a lot of time on studying human consciousness, believing strongly that the unconscious mind is a place where important events take place. Returning to the iceberg metaphor, he suggested that the unconscious is what lies deeply hidden in the water, below the surface.

He believed, this being confirmed by modern researchers and psychoanalysts, that the unconscious mind is a place where we hide various things. If you have ever had an idea which might have been perceived as socially unacceptable, it is highly likely that idea was stored in the unconscious. The same goes for unfulfilled wishes or desires, for any memories related to traumas or any emotion which the brain might have perceived as too painful. Out of mind, out of sight. This is the phenomenon of psychological repression.

Perhaps as a form of protection, all the things that are stored in the unconscious mind are not available for us to analyze them. However, psychoanalysts, such as Sigmund Freud, have always tried to tap into the unconscious, in order to reveal essential information about the human psyche. Methods such as dream analysis, meditation and even the interpretation of tongue slips, have been used since the dawn of modern psychoanalysis, in order to draw information from the unconscious part of mind.

Sigmund Freud paid particular attention to the tongue slips, considering these to be the best way to tap into the unconscious mind. In the opinion of the psychoanalyst, it was through the slips of the tongue, that other people revealed their true views on certain things.

Other specialists and their views on the unconscious mind

Freud was the one to begin the true research into the world of human personality and its three levels, believing that the unconscious mind is mainly responsible for the way people behave. However, he would not remain the only one to exhibit a curiosity for such matters, with other specialists, such as Carl Jung and Jacques Lacan threading in his footsteps.

Carl Jung shared some of his friend's views on the unconscious mind but he took his research further, coming up with his own version. According to the Swiss physician, the unconscious mind was a clear determinant of one's personality, with the distinction that it could be divided into two categories, meaning the personal and the collective.

The research performed by Carl Jung revealed that the unconscious mind contained indeed our basic instincts, meaning those related to sex and aggression. However, it was our rational self, the conscious mind, which prevented these from being transported into reality. Based on the research at that point, it was concluded that the unconscious mind was actually a shadow of the conscious mind.

Jacques Lacan, a French psychoanalyst, exhibited an interest in the structure of the mind as well. His contribution to the psychoanalyst theory of the mind was based on the idea that the unconscious was actually structured like a language. Lacan wanted for other specialists of his time to understand that the unconscious mind was not primitive or archetypal but just as complex and sophisticated at the rest of the mind structures. This is why he compared its complexity to the one of a language.

Is the unconscious mind Pandora's box?

In Greek mythology, we are told about the story of Zeus, king of all gods and the way he gave Pandora, the first mortal woman, a box. Pandora received specific instructions never to open that box but, at the same time, she was given the gift of curiosity. Because of this gift, she could not help opening the box, thus releasing misery and perils on all of mankind. So, if we were to think for a moment, the comparison of the unconscious mind with Pandora's Box is quite obvious. Everything we have repressed is hidden in the unconscious mind and it is up to us, whether we let it out or not.

Modern views on the unconscious mind

Even though a long time has passed since Sigmund Freud's researches, the unconscious mind is still a subject of interest for today's modern psychoanalysts. Numerous studies are being undertaken, in order to determine the role of the unconscious mind and how it influences the conscious and subconscious structures. For example, it was recently discovered that people who are engaged in a regular meditation, are also more in tune with the unconscious part of their mind.

The unconscious mind will, no doubt, continue to puzzle scientists for many years to come. Despite the extensive research, there are many things we still do not know about the unconscious and many more that we need to clarify.

Food for thought

1) Why do you think some people give in to their primitive urges? What role does the unconscious mind play in this case?

2) What is connection between the unconscious mind and human behavior?

3) Are the views of Sigmund Freud valid today? Or has new research changed the perception regarding the unconscious mind?

Chapter 4 – The power of thoughts

Anonymous: "If you realized how powerful your thoughts are, you would never think a negative thought."

We never tend to pay too much attention to our thoughts, up to the point when we realize that they have a definite impact on the way we view life. Even the smallest thought can change the course of your life, impacting your behavior and attitude. Once you learn how to control your thoughts and steer them in the right direction, it is guaranteed you will reach the point you want in life and enjoy it to the fullest.

Be careful about what you think

A wise person once said that thoughts are the architects of one's destiny. That is quite true, especially if you stop for a moment and think, how big of a difference positive thinking can actually make in a person's life.

In order to understand the power of thoughts, let's take a practical analogy. Imagine your thoughts as being part of a video, playing on the screen of your mind. If the video includes only negative parts, this will be a determinant of the life you are going to lead and the experiences you are going to encounter. So, before you decide to change your life, change your way of thinking. Switch to a video which is more positive and good changes will subsequently follow into your life.

You can train yourself to think positively

It all starts with one positive thought. Then, with the right amount of training, you will actually make that thought stronger and attract others, equally positive. Once you get accustomed to positive thinking, you can use it to attract the things you want in life and influence other people, into thinking positively as well.

Imagine, if you will, that you have a garden. You have taken your time to plant a wide range of seeds and now you spend a generous amount of time, watering and caring for them. Soon, if all goes well, you will have plants that are both healthy and strong. Well, you can easily understand that thoughts are exactly like seeds. If you plant positive thoughts in your mind, taking your time to cultivate them, it is highly likely you will lead a great life as well.

Always remember that thoughts, whether positive or negative, are passed on from the conscious to the subconscious mind. The latter will work really hard to determine your actions and overall behavior, in accordance with such thoughts. As you will have the opportunity to read below, it is possible to train yourself to think positively, especially with the help of visualization.

Life determines thoughts and the other way around

Each day, you come into contact with a number of people. You experience a wide range of things, read various content and form new perceptions. All of these things are stored in your mind, leading to the formation of thoughts. From a simple perspective, it would be simple to say that, if you have negative experiences and only come in contact with negative people, your thoughts are going to be negative as well. On the other hand, a positive life experience also leads to positive thoughts.

This is a rather simplistic view on life and quite far from the truth. Regardless of the experiences you have, it is still up to you to decide, whether you are going to transport them inside your mind (positive or negative thinking). You are the master of your own destiny and this is why you get to decide, which thoughts are worth keeping and which ones should be instantly removed, as they are weighing you down. Surely, this will take some time and a lot of effort but, in the end, it will be all worth it.

Use the power of thoughts to change your life

Keep in mind that the way you think can influence even your body and the way it responds to certain situations. People who are too hard on themselves, as well as those who are excessively judgmental, will often experience negative thoughts, with the subconscious mind working to reduce their overall self-esteem. On the other hand, if you think in a positive manner and take some pressure off yourself, you will see that these positive thoughts are also transported into positive actions.

A piece of bad news can change your life forever, especially if your mind is prone to negative thinking. There are people who, upon hearing that they suffer from a terminal illness and they will die within several months, they actually die within that period. This is because the mind has integrated that thought, influencing the biology of the body and its subsequent behavior. In the field of cellular biology, this is known as the nocebo effect, which is caused by a pattern of negative thinking. This appears in contrast with the placebo effect, which is known to be influence by positive thoughts.

Are you an optimist or a pessimist?

From what has been said so far, you have probably understood that your thoughts influence your journey in real life. So, if you want to make a change, you need to begin with your way of thinking.

It was once said that it is impossible for a person not be aware of his/her own thoughts, especially since they are so influential on outside life. This is the reason why you have complete liberty to decide, if you want to look at life from an optimist's perspective or you want to think like a pessimist (glass half empty).

It might interest you to know that the majority of the people out there are prone to negative thinking. However, this does not mean that all people let themselves be conquered by these negative thoughts. In fact, the most successful people out there acknowledge these negative thoughts and they work really hard to challenge, rather than accept them.

What you need to do is educate yourself, to become more aware of the pattern of thinking you are currently experiencing. Do not become obsessed with your thoughts but rather adjust them in a positive direction, as this will guarantee a positive mental attitude overall and success in real life.

In the situation that negative thoughts ramble through your mind, learn how to instantly neutralize them. Use positive thinking and replace any negative thought with its alternate, positive version. For example, instead of thinking that you are not good enough for a job or that you will never achieve the success you dreamt of, repeat to yourself that you are actually good enough for that job and that you will achieve success. This will be a life changing experience and one that will get you on the path of positive thinking.

Food for thought

1) Are you an optimist or pessimist?

2) How big of an influence do you believe thoughts have on our behavior and general perspective on life?

3) Definite positive and negative thinking in your own words.

Chapter 5 – Visualization

Anonymous: "If you can imagine it and visualize it, you can create it."

Visualization is often presented in conjunction with mind power, representing the best mental exercise you can try, in order to achieve or obtain the things you want. It all starts with you imagining that you have already obtained whatever it was that you wanted in the first place. The more you go through the process, the higher your chance of actually succeeding in real life.

Imagination, a key element of visualization

Your mind is more powerful than you think, with imagination playing a key role in the whole visualization business. All you have to do is close your eyes and imagine yourself successful. Or, depending on the things you are interested in, you can imagine yourself closing a business deal, finding the love of your life and healing existent wounds. What you wish for does not matter, what matters is that you are able to visualize yourself already at that final point.

At the beginning, you might be tempted to only hope for the things you want to achieve, without actually picturing yourself succeeding. However, the trick is to visualize yourself, successful and at exactly at the point you wanted. Do not just try to build your confidence and hope that, some day, everything will fall into place. Instead, use your imagination to experience achieving the things you want, taking advantage of your brain and its susceptibility to visualization.

Don't think that your brain has simply failed to acknowledge that you are playing a trick on it. However, what happens is that the subconscious mind cannot actually make the difference between reality and imagination. This is why, if you go over the same mental images, repeating the process on a daily basis, you will force your brain to work in that direction. Reality has very little to do with it, which is great.

Visualization techniques

1) Daydreaming with a purpose

This is one of the simplest visualization techniques, one that has been a valuable weapon of businessmen, professional athletes and other important people out there, for a long period of time. This visualization technique, based on the mental imagery of your success, can help you develop strength, self-esteem and confidence, all at once.

It might interest you to know that this technique can help you get through difficult situations, such as important presentations, conferences or other such events. All you want to do is imagine yourself, from zero to the final point, exactly as you would desire for things to turn out. In this way, you will be able to better focus on the actual presentation, enjoying the improved performance. Once again, this technique is effective, simply because our brain can be easily tricked, in getting involved in imaginary situations (in a similar manner to real life).

2) Write it down

If you are the kind who likes to express himself/herself through writing, this visualization technique might be more useful than you might think. Imagine the things you want to achieve and write the story of your success. Take your time to describe the whole process in detail, making sure that you cherish in every small step you have successfully achieved (even if, at this point, this is only a story). This will help you stay focused and fight hard to actually enjoy that story in real life.

3) Step-by-step

Sometimes, it's not enough to imagine yourself having succeeded. You need to break up that success into smaller milestones, taking step-by-step. Let's say you have to give a presentation and you are really nervous about it. Begin by imagining the conference room, paying attention to even the smallest details, such as lighting, ambient temperature and the clothes you are wearing.

Take a deep breath and proceed, imaging yourself delivering the presentation. However, do not imagine a 100% perfect presentation, as in real life, things might not go as planned. Instead, imagine yourself overcoming small mistakes and other potential difficulties, striving to imagine the best possible presentation you would give in reality as well.

4) Drawing

Like many other visualization techniques, this particular one requires both your mental and physical involvement. The first thing that you want to do is think about something you want to achieve, such as, for example, successfully passing an important exam.

Disregard your drawing talent and take a sheet of paper, drawing the building in which you are going to take the exam, room, yourself and other elements involved in the process (exam papers, colleagues, teachers). Imagine yourself going through the exam with success, using your drawing to visualize the road towards your objective.

5) Movie

For this technique, imagine yourself, as if you were watching a movie in your head. The big difference is that you are in control of the movie scenes, as if you were the director. While this is not a visualization technique as active as the others, it can still be highly effective and definitely worth trying.

What you want to do is choose a quiet room, with no distractions whatsoever (loud noises, other people etc.). Lie on your back, close your eyes and go through the scenes. Once you have obtained a sequence and you know exactly what you want to achieve, you can go ahead and introduce additional details, such as other people, sounds and smells. Slowly build the movie of your success, making sure that you are in the center of attention.

6) Altering of memories

This is one of the most interesting visualization techniques out there, allowing you to change negative memories. You can use this technique, in order to give a positive spin, on a memory which you perceive as hurtful or sad. This is especially recommended to those who have a lot of memories involving hatred or malice.

What you want to do is go over that memory again, no matter how difficult this might prove out to be. Then, replace the sad or negative part with a positive reaction; if it is not possible to be positive, then at least try to be calm and in control of the situation. This will take some time but, in the end, your brain will only remember the positive memory, the other one fading away.

Food for thought

1) Have you ever used visualization? Give one example.

2) Why is it difficult for the brain to distinguish between real-life and imagined situations?

3) Use one of the visualization techniques and see how it works for a practical situation.

Chapter 6 – Mind power and the law of attraction

Richard Bach: "To bring anything into your life, imagine that it's already there."

Mind power and the law of attraction

We have often read about the law of attraction and how the universe always gives exactly what you put out there. Used in conjunction with the power of thoughts, the law of attraction can help you obtain everything you have always wanted.

The most important thing to remember is that the conscious mind is initially responsible for our thoughts. Once these appear, they are automatically transferred to the subconscious. The more we believe certain things, the deeper they will be embedded into the subconscious. Because, whether you are aware of this for a fact or not, the subconscious will accept all of your thoughts, good or bad, positive or negative. Both real and imagined things will be accepted by the subconscious as valid, as it will fight to help you achieve them.

Let's take a practical example, in order to understand the deep connection between mind power and the law of attraction. If you wake up one morning and say to yourself this is going to be a bad day, the universe will give you exactly that. Then, your day will go badly, reinforcing the power of your subconscious. On the other hand, if you think positively and say to yourself that you are going to have a great day, the universe will work to attract the things and circumstances you desire. Always be mindful of your thoughts and their incredible power, as they can make the difference between being happiness and leading a miserable existence.

More on the law of attraction

The universe responds to our thoughts and sends to us exactly what we wish for. When we make a conscious effort, to think positive thoughts, the universe will send back positive energy. However, such a belief system requires a lot of patience, until those nasty, negative thoughts are kept down to a minimum.

Whenever you think positive thoughts, you are sending a success vibration in the universe. This will act in a similar manner with a magnet, attracting the things you have wanted in the first place. Successful people have this powerful belief system deep embedded in their subconscious; apart from the conscious efforts they make, in order to reach their objectives, they also think and feel successful.

Take a good look at people who have already achieved success and you will easily understand how the law of attraction has worked for them. You will always attract success and opportunities by thinking in a positive manner.

Acknowledging technique

If you are not successful yet, there is a technique that you can try, in order to accustom yourself to positive thinking and, thus, attract the much-desired success. This is known as the acknowledging technique and it requires that you take a good look at your life, finding the areas in which you have already succeeded. In this way, you will obtain a more positive outlook on life, sending a success vibration into the universe and, thus, attracting positive things and circumstances. This might take some time, because, like the majority of the people out there, we are more inclined to see the areas in which we have yet to succeed rather than the ones in which we are successful already.

How does the law of attraction function?

As it was already mentioned above, you attract the things that correspond to your predominant thoughts. Every aspect of your life is influenced by the law of attraction and both your conscious and subconscious mind work to help you come in harmony with the universe.

People, along with their thoughts, are pure energy. Each and every thought is sent out into the universe, representing a wave of energy. Interestingly enough, each thought you put out there, vibrates at a different frequency. The law of attraction is simple: energy attracts energy. However, it does matter on which frequency your thoughts are and whether these are in harmony with the universe or not.

According to the law of attraction, you will always attract what corresponds to your thoughts, not necessarily what you should deserve in the first place. Your mental attitude has a clear influence on the ability to attract positive things, with the subconscious mind hiding not only your thoughts but also habitual beliefs. Simply put, a positive mental attitude will attract positive things; a negative one, negative things.

How can you attract the things you want?

Your mind is the most powerful instrument you will ever possess; used correctly, it can help you attract the things you want. What matters is that you think positively, as this will help you attract positive energy and reach the point you want in life. Don't think that you are not connected to the universe because, as a human being, you are a source of pure energy and always connected to the big world out there.

The law of attraction can be used in a conscious manner. What you want to do is train your thoughts and send success vibrations, thus entering into vibrational harmony with the great universe out there. In order to attract positive things, you can use a technique known as creative visualization. We have spoken about visualization in the chapter above, so you can go ahead and give it another read. Creative visualization can help you reprogram the subconscious mind and change your mindset into a positive one.

Word of advice

Whenever something goes wrong or we fail to achieve the things we desire for, we have the tendency of blaming ourselves for our failures. In some situations, we may go as far as placing the blame on others, considering that our life would have been better, if it wasn't for them. However, you should never waste your energy in placing the blame on someone, but rather think about the power of thoughts and the law of attraction. Work consciously to change your mental attitude and think more positively. Soon, you will see how much your life has changed, obviously, for the better.

Food for thought

1) Name one positive thought and its negative version. Analyze the difference.

2) Do you think that the law of attraction functions the same for everyone out there?

3) Comment on the affirmation: "What you think, you create".

Chapter 7 – Mind power myths

Aneta Cruz: "Your mind is your greatest power. Use it well."

Nowadays, there are a lot of people – inspirational speakers, psychologists and other experts – who speak about mind power. We are given access to a wealth of information, coming from a wide range of sources and, sometimes, it can be difficult to point out which facts are true and which are closer to fiction. You might not be aware of it but there are a number of myths associated with mind power. We have taken the time to present some of them, so go ahead and read about the most common myths and misconceptions regarding the power of thoughts.

#1 Myth: The subconscious mind will absorb all information in a straight pattern, resembling a movie

The idea that the subconscious mind records all information, similar to a movie, has been perpetuated by numerous scientists and experts out there. Based on this idea, it was suggested that people can remember any event from their past, without any difficulty (perfect clarity). However, this is only a myth. As early as the 1930s, it was demonstrated that the subconscious mind registers information according to a schema. This is actually a cluster of pre-conceived notions, engulfing our habitual beliefs, thoughts and actions. Interestingly enough, it was discovered that memories are often changed, in order to fit our pre-conceived notions (and, thus, maintain the same image about the world itself, according to our own pattern of thought).

#2 Myth: Only 10% of the brain capacity is actively being used

The notion that humans only use 10% of their brain capacity has been discussed, commented upon and analyzed by various health experts. However, according to the latest research, it has proven out to be nothing more than a myth. Brain scans, performed with modern-generation MRI machines, have proven that we use a large portion of the brain, if not all, in accordance to the activities we are involved in. Depending on the said activity, it is possible that areas responsible for hearing, seeing, memorizing, thinking and interpreting are active at the same time. This is because all areas in the brain are connected, working in close collaboration, in order to ensure our best possible functioning.

#3 Myth: Sleep learning is possible

We live in a world where a lot of people are making a living, by selling self-help products and miracle therapies. Many of these people support the idea that sleep learning is a possible matter. However, it was as early as the 1950s, that a teach of scientists used EEG recordings and demonstrated that the brain cannot accumulate information, while in sleep mode. In order for the information to be absorbed and sent to the subconscious mind, the actual learning would have to occur before going to sleep.

When we sleep, new connections form at the level of the brain. Even on sleep mode, the brain is highly active but not in the way you might imagine. Based on the information you accumulate in an entire day, it will have to accomplish the hard job of deciding what data should be kept and passed on to the subconscious mind. At the same time, the rest of the information will be sent to the trash bin, clearing your mind for the next day. So, bottom line, if you are asleep, it means that neither the conscious, nor the subconscious mind, can perceive new information.

#4 Myth: Subliminal messages influence our decisions

Subliminal messages are often used by mass media and also by various companies, who are trying to convince us to purchase their products and/or services. Governments and large organizations resort to subliminal messages, in order to change the public opinion, regarding various actions or changes. But are these actually capable of affecting our decisions?

In the 1950s, at the beginning of the cinema era, a study was undertaken, in order to reveal how powerful subliminal messages actually were. When a movie started, the viewers were shown a series of images, with the message "hungry for popcorn?" The authors of the study stated that the sales of popcorn increased in viewers who had seen those messages. However, at a short time after the results of the study were published, it was revealed that the data was false.

While it is true that a subliminal message is meant to reach our subconscious and influence our behavior, this rarely happens. Imagine listening to those tapes that are supposed to help you quit smoking. This might help you to get to sleep faster but, with regard to smoking, your subconscious mind is more powerful than any subliminal message. Think about that.

#5 Myth: Unrealistic expectations are given by positive thinking

Positive thinking is considered, by some people, the source of unrealistic experience. Not only this is a false assumption but, at a closer look, you will definitely discover that you stand to gain a lot by adopting a positive mindset. If you were to look at some of the most famous speeches held by inspirational speakers, with regard to positive thinking, you would find out that the most important thing is to acknowledge your real desires.

Surely, you might believe that you are doing this every day. But, in reality, very few of us dedicate the deserved amount of time to this process. It's not enough to repeat that we are satisfied with what we have at the moment; in order to reach the desired point in life, we must ask ourselves, in an honest manner, what we really want. In this way, we might reach to interesting conclusions and decide to make beneficial changes.

Food for thought

1) Can you name another myth regarding mind power?

2) Can the subconscious mind be influenced by subliminal messages? If yes, to what extent?

3) Are there any downsides to positive thinking?

Chapter 8 – Subconscious mind power techniques

Earl Nightingale: "Whatever we plant in our subconscious mind and nourish with repetition and emotion will one day become a reality."

The subconscious mind is an integral part of who you are and more important than you might think. It is active at all times, without being actually conscious of its presence. The interesting thing is that subconscious mind holds all the power of bringing changes in your life. It represents the internal drive, which determines whether you will be successful or not. The good news is that there are a number of techniques, which you can use to train your subconscious mind and achieve the things you have always dreamt about.

#1 Problem solving

You might not be aware of this for a fact but you can actually train your subconscious mind, especially when it comes to solving problems, for which you cannot find an actual solution. What you need to do is take some time and think about the problem you are facing. If you like to express yourself in writing, you can go ahead and write it down. In this way, you will transfer the responsibility of finding a solution, from the conscious to the subconscious mind.

The subconscious mind will gladly accept the responsibility and will work on finding the best solution to your problem. This is why you need to stop thinking about the problem and concentrate on every day activities. Soon, you will see that the solution appears in front of your eyes, with the subconscious mind being responsible for the epiphany.

#2 Meditation

Meditation is one of the most powerful ways in which you can train your subconscious and develop mind power. Performed on a regular basis, it helps you become more focused. Once you reach a higher level of concentration, you will find it easier to achieve your goals. In a beautiful way, meditation allows you to get in touch with your deeper self, discovering things you never thought were possible.

Used by people from various cultures and all around the world, meditation remains one of the most efficient techniques for communicating with the subconscious mind. The more you meditate, the easier it will be to reach that part of yourself. The most important thing is that you meditate in a quiet environment, with few or, if possible no distractions. As you become accustomed to the meditation process, you can incorporate positive affirmations or visualization into your daily ritual.

#3 Repeated visualization

This is one of the most efficient visualization techniques and one that can definitely help you train your subconscious mind, gearing it towards the right direction. If there ever was a method to help you achieve your goals, you should definitely consider repeated visualization, as it is highly efficient.

What you need to do is think really well about the things you want to achieve. Let your imagination run free and do not set limits, but rather spend your time putting your passion into real actions. Set some time aside each and every day, in order to think about the big objective and the pathway that you need to follow, so as to achieve it. The subconscious mind will not distinguish between things imagined and those that are real, working really hard to help you achieve your goals.

#4 Positive words

When you educate yourself to use positive words, it becomes easier and easier to change your mindset and get rid of beliefs that are actually limiting you. You will see how great it can be to associate a positive word with a similar feeling, thus making a complete turn in your life. At first, you might experience certain difficulties, as the majority of us are concentrated on negative thoughts. However, with dedication and discipline, you will definitely discover the power of positive words and the great influence they have over the subconscious mind.

Positive words, as well as affirmations, can help you reprogram the subconscious mind. The more you use them, the easier it will be for your subconscious mind to get rid of negative thoughts and help you achieve the things you want. For example, if you constantly repeat to yourself the word "happiness", this will be accepted and integrated into the subconscious mind.

#5 Will & habit

Will refers to the way we decide to respond to a particular situation, with two possibilities lying in front of us: passive and active responding. When we say habit, we speak about a behavior that we have formed in time and which now has become part of the daily routine (we not conscious about it). These two processes share a deep connection and you can use them to reprogram your subconscious mind. Watch out for the way you respond to given situations, as well as to the way you integrate new behaviors and transform them into habits (make a conscious effort).

#6 Self-suggestion

Self-suggestion is a simple method that can be used to reprogram the subconscious mind but only at first sight. You get to tell the subconscious mind about the things you would like to achieve but it will take a lot of time and plenty of repetition, in order for things to sink in. This is why you should not quit and use self suggestions on a daily basis. At some point, your subconscious mind will accept your suggestions and begin working towards your set objectives.

Final word

So, you see, there are a number of ways, in which you can reprogram your subconscious mind and make a positive change in your life. As you have seen for yourself, these techniques require perseverance and dedication, so make sure to work really hard and train your subconscious mind the right way.

Food for thought

1) Can you name other techniques that can be used to reprogram the subconscious mind?

2) How are will and habit connected?

3) How susceptible do you think the subconscious mind is to self suggestion?

Chapter 9 – Practical tips to stimulate the power of the mind

David Cuschieri: "The mind is a powerful force. It can enslave us or empower us. It can plunge us into the depths of misery or take us to the heights of ecstasy. Learn to use that power wisely."

We cannot separate ourselves from our mind, as it is one of the most defining parts of who we are. However, it can happen that we forget, how important our mind actually is and how big an influence it can have on our exterior lives. The good news is that we can stimulate the power of the mind, in order to make a positive change in our lives and obtain everything we have always dreamt of.

#1 Go for new experiences

In many ways, the brain resembles a muscle, requiring constant training, in order to stay fit. If you want to stimulate your mind power, you have to open yourself up to new experiences. Learn something new each day, avoid getting such in a routine and, in this way, you will create additional neural pathways towards the subconscious mind. Even simple things, like preparing a new type of food, changing your route to work or meeting a new person, can make a huge difference.

#2 Physical exercise

When you engage in physical exercise on a regular basis, you are actually getting an excellent workout for the mind as well. This is because physical training has been shown to stimulate neural pathways, leading to the formation of brain cells. So, the next time you feel like rather staying at home, you might want to consider getting a nice workout. Your mind will definitely welcome this decision, becoming stronger with every day that passes.

#3 Allow yourself to be curious

Being curious is one of the easiest ways to stimulate your mind power, not to mention fun. Every day, we take a lot of things for granted, without necessarily questioning why they are in a particular way. When you begin to question things, this is a good thing, especially for your mind. It loves nothing more than having the opportunity to discover new things, even if they come to crash with some of the pre-conceived notions you might have stored in your brain. Forget about people who say that curiosity is not a good thing and think about all the innovations that come from people who listened to their intuition.

#4 Positive thinking

When you think in a positive manner, you open yourself to an entire world of possibilities. On the other hand, negative thinking, combined with stress and anxiety, can actually prevent you from seeing exactly what was in front of you. The more you train yourself to think positively, the easier it will be to see new possibilities and, thus, increase your mind power. It is like a vicious circle and you need to put a stop to all those negative thoughts, making a conscious effort to replace them with positive ones.

#5 Healthy eating

You might not expect the diet to be one of the best ways to stimulate your mind but it actually is. Our mind requires a lot of nutrients, in order to function at its absolute best, so make sure to pay attention to the things you are eating. Include plenty of fresh fruits and veggies in your daily diet, as well as fatty fish and nuts. All of these will help your mind stay sharp, especially the fatty fish and nuts, which are rich in beneficial omega-3 and omega-6 fatty acids.

#6 Reading

Reading is a favorite pastime for a lot of people but not many of them are aware of how useful such an activity actually is. This activity not only stimulates your mind but, at the same time, it relieves the stress and tension, which might have led to negative thinking. The mind is highly active during reading, trying to imagine the scenarios in the book and, thus, gaining more and more power. Plus, it's quite fun to read, discovering several worlds at once!

#7 Sleep for 7-8 hours per night

If you are tired, you cannot expect your brain to function at its maximum capacity. In order to keep a sharp mind and impress everyone with your mind power, you need to sleep, at least 7-8 hours per night. Sleeping allows the brain to accumulate information, forming new pathways, which are highly beneficial for the mind in general. If you get accustomed to sleeping the recommended amount of hours each night, you will definitely enjoy your mind, at its absolute best capacity.

#8 Read a map

Whenever we are going on a travel, we tend to use the navigator of the car and reach the destination in comfort. However, in the old days, traveling meant reading a map, looking at signs and stopping to ask for directions, if such a thing was necessary. Map reading might become an obsolete thing in the near future but you cannot even begin to imagine, how beneficial it is for the mind. When you take your time to read a map, your mind is actively involved in finding the best route, enjoying the challenge.

#9 Memory training

Smartphones, as well as other devices, have made us lazy. They keep all the information for us, including phone numbers, doctor appointments and things to do. Unfortunately, this does not have a positive effect on our minds, causing us to lose an important ability and that is the one to memorize information. Memory training can help you stimulate your mind power at the same time, so make sure you give it a try. Begin by memorizing important phone numbers, force yourself to keep track of doctor appointments and play memory games, as these can be of big help as well.

#10 Do math the old way

If you have to calculate certain figures or numbers, you are definitely going to resort to your computer. However, this is another thing which puts a damp on our minds, causing us to rely on external devices rather than on us. The next time you need to perform certain calculations, take a sheet of paper and do the math the old way. At first, you might be tempted to take your computer and get things done faster. Nevertheless, you need to resist the temptation and use your own mind, as this is the best kind of training you can get yourself engaged in.

As you can see, there are plenty of ways, in which you can stimulate your mind power and open yourself up to an entire world, filled with new and exciting possibilities.

Food for thought

1) Can you name three other ways in which you can stimulate your mind power?

2) Has our mind power changed, as we are living in the age of technology?

3) Why does negative thinking impair mind power?

Chapter 10 – The subconscious mind, a partner for success

Napoleon Hill: "The starting point of all achievement is desire. Keep this constantly in mind. Weak desire brings weak results, just as a small amount of fire makes a small amount of heat."

Your mind is one of the most important resources you have available, especially with regard to succeeding in life. However, in order to turn your subconscious mind into a partner for success, it is essential that you stop all that negative thinking and work consciously to steer yourself towards positive thoughts. In this way, you will establish the foundation for success, achieving all the things you have ever wanted.

What are the things that the subconscious mind responds to?

First and foremost, you need to understand that we all have the potential to be successful, as long as we feed the subconscious mind with the right things.

In order to awaken the subconscious mind and thread the path towards success, you must take into consideration the influence of outside factors on your own thoughts. Think about the fact that the subconscious mind is easily influenced by repeated thoughts, as well as by various stimuli. You cannot hope to be successful, without learning how to respond to the environment and its associated factors.

The subconscious mind can respond to a wide range of stimuli, including music, movies, books and human interaction in particular. You should always pay attention to these things – the songs that you listen on the radio, the movies you watch at the TV and the books that come across you. Last, but not least, if you want to achieve all of your objectives and taste the sweet nectar of success, you need to surround yourself with people who are on a similar level with you. And, remember, the subconscious mind is the one in control of your behavior, so it is up to you to influence it and gear it towards the right direction.

How can you steer the subconscious mind in the direction of success?

One of the easiest ways to steer the subconscious mind in the direction of success is visualization. All you have to do is imagine yourself in the desired situation, making sure that you are as relaxed as you possibly can.

Always visualize the goal you want to achieve, as if it were real, as the subconscious mind cannot make the difference between what is real and what is imagined. Use all of your senses, in order to create a complex picture and add as many details you feel like.

When you visualize yourself achieving the things you want, the subconscious mind is encouraged to work for those things and come up with innovative solutions. The most important thing is that you are consistent, visualizing your desired goal(s) each and every day, until they become actual reality. Interestingly enough, the subconscious mind will work, not only to help you identify opportunities that come across your way but also to draw attention to things you might have failed to see in the first place.

Let's take a practical example, in order to understand how this process of guided imagery functions. The first thing that you need to do is find a quiet room, choosing a relaxed position. Next, breathe in and out, so as to become even more relaxed and let go of all worries. Now, it is time to think about a goal that you want to achieve. This can be anything, from closing a business deal to finding the love of your life. Guide yourself through the process and imagine finally achieving that objective.

Give a multitude of details to that final scene, thinking about what it feels like, what are your actions in the moment and your exact position. Add sounds, smells and people you are interacting with. This kind of mental rehearsal is more beneficial than you might think, especially when repeated on a regular basis. Surely, this kind of exercise takes a lot of time and discipline, so do not be disappointed if you do not get it right the first time. Keep in mind that practice makes perfect, so be sure to repeat it, each and every day.

If visualization does not do it for you, you can go ahead and give positive affirmations a try. This technique has been explained in chapters above but, with regard to training the subconscious mind for success, there is one thing you might want to opt for. Try these positive affirmations before going to sleep, as this is when the subconscious mind is most open to suggestions.

When you are preparing to fall sleep, the conscious mind is experiencing tiredness, letting its guard down. Because that, it will be less active in questioning your affirmations. This is when you need to step in and fill your subconscious mind with positive affirmations. You can also combine these positive affirmations with meditation, in order to increase their overall power.

Food for thought

1) Can you define the connection between the subconscious mind and success?

2) Is success reserved only for certain people?

3) Why does the conscious mind fight out affirmations?

Conclusion

This book delivers a complex view on mind power, allowing you to finally understand how big of a role the subconscious mind plays in our lives. It takes you through the three essential structures of the mind, revealing essential information on the functions of the conscious mind, the power of the subconscious and the repression associated with the unconscious.

As you go through the chapters of the book, you are able to discover how important each and every thought is. You are face-to-face with commonly used visualization techniques, practicing them by yourself. The reading experience allows you to discover the connection between mind power and the law of attraction, as well as how to use them at the same time, in order to achieve the things you always dreamt of.

You are given the opportunity to discover some of the most common myths regarding mind power, so that you get a clear view regarding some matters. You move on and discover subconscious mind power techniques, which are definitely going to come in handy in real life. The same goes for the practical tips to stimulate the power of the mind, as these can be easily transferred into real life. Last, but not least, you are taught how to use the subconscious mind and transform it in your partner for success.

Use this book to make a positive change in your life and start working today for the things that you want to achieve. Remember that your mind is the most important tool you will ever have available and that you can train it in an efficient manner, so that it works in your interest and not against you.

Made in the USA
Las Vegas, NV
25 November 2022

60307886R00022